Social Media Security: Protecting Your Digital Life

C. P. Kumar
Reiki Healer
Roorkee - 247667, India

DEDICATION

To all the individuals who have fallen victim to cybercrimes and online attacks, and to those who value their privacy and security in the digital world. May this book serve as a guide to help you protect your digital life and navigate the Wild West of social media.

C. P. Kumar

CONTENTS

PREFACE

Social media has become an integral part of our daily lives. It is where we connect with friends and family, share our personal and professional experiences, and even conduct business transactions. However, as the popularity of social media continues to grow, so do the risks and threats associated with it. From identity theft and phishing scams to cyberbullying and online harassment, social media security is a complex and ever-evolving issue.

This book, "Social Media Security: Protecting Your Digital Life," is a comprehensive guide to help you understand the risks and threats associated with social media and how to protect yourself and your business from them. The book is divided into 20 chapters, each of which focuses on a different aspect of social media security.

The first chapter, "Introduction: The Wild West of Social Media," sets the stage by highlighting the rapid growth of social media and the lack of regulation and oversight that has led to a host of security issues. The subsequent chapters delve into the specifics of social media security, including privacy settings, password management, phishing and identity theft, common social media scams, online harassment, and reputation management.

The later chapters of the book explore the complex and rapidly evolving world of social media security, including emerging threats and trends, the role of artificial intelligence and machine learning in social media security, and the legal implications of social media fraud and impersonation. Real-life case studies of social media scams and impersonation are also included to illustrate the real-world consequences of poor social media security practices.

This book is not only intended for individuals looking to protect their personal and professional social media presence but also for social media managers, businesses, and parents looking to keep themselves and their families safe online. The comprehensive and practical advice provided in this book will help you take control of your social media security and protect yourself from the myriad of risks and threats associated with it.

We hope you find this book informative and useful in navigating the complex world of social media security.

C. P. Kumar
Reiki Healer
Former Scientist 'G', National Institute of Hydrology
Roorkee - 247667, India
E-mail: cpkumar@yahoo.com
Web: https://www.angelfire.com/nh/cpkumar/virgo.html

Chapter 1. Introduction: The Wild West of Social Media

Introduction

The internet has revolutionized the way we communicate and interact with one another. Social media platforms have made it easier than ever before to connect with people from all over the world, to share our thoughts and opinions, and to stay up-to-date on the latest news and trends. However, with this newfound freedom and accessibility has come a new set of challenges, as social media has become the Wild West of our time, where anything goes and the rules are constantly changing.

In this article, we will explore the Wild West of social media, examining the challenges that come with this new frontier, the impact of social media on our society, and the potential solutions that could help tame this untamed landscape.

The Challenges of the Wild West

One of the biggest challenges of the Wild West of social media is the lack of regulation. Unlike traditional forms of media, social media is largely unregulated, meaning that anyone can post anything they like, regardless of its accuracy or the potential harm it may cause. This has led to a number of problems, including the spread of misinformation, hate speech, and cyberbullying.

Another challenge is the sheer volume of content that is posted on social media platforms every day. With billions of users around the world, social media platforms are inundated with content, making it difficult to police and monitor for inappropriate or harmful content.

Finally, social media algorithms themselves can contribute to the Wild West mentality. Social media platforms often prioritize content that generates the most engagement, regardless of its accuracy or impact, incentivizing users to create controversial or clickbait content that can be harmful to society.

The Impact of Social Media on Society

The Wild West of social media has had a profound impact on society, both positive and negative. On the positive side, social media has made it easier than ever before to connect with people from all over the world. It has given marginalized groups a platform to speak out and has facilitated the exchange of ideas and information on a global scale.

However, the negative impact of social media cannot be ignored. Social media has been linked to a number of negative outcomes, including increased rates of depression and anxiety, decreased social skills, and the spread of harmful and false information.

One of the most significant negative impacts of social media is the spread of misinformation. Social media platforms have been used to spread conspiracy theories, propaganda, and false information, often with disastrous consequences. This has led to a widespread mistrust of traditional sources of information, such as the media and government, and has contributed to a climate of fear and uncertainty.

Another negative impact of social media is the spread of hate speech and cyberbullying. Social media platforms have become a breeding ground for hate speech and harassment, with users often using anonymity to hide behind their words. This can lead to real-world consequences, such as increased rates of suicide and self-harm.

Potential Solutions

Taming the Wild West of social media will require a multi-faceted approach that addresses the challenges outlined above. One potential solution is increased regulation of social media platforms. Governments and regulatory bodies could set standards for the type of content that is allowed on social media platforms, with penalties for platforms that fail to comply.

Another solution is increased transparency from social media platforms themselves. Platforms could be required to disclose how their algorithms work and how they prioritize content, giving users more insight into how their data is being used.

Finally, education is key to taming the Wild West of social media. Users need to be educated on how to spot and avoid false information, how to engage with others in a respectful and constructive way, and how to protect themselves from online harassment and cyberbullying.

Conclusion

The Wild West of social media has given us unprecedented freedom and access to information, but it has also created new challenges that must be addressed if we are to create a safe and healthy online environment. From the spread of misinformation and hate speech to the negative impact on mental health, the Wild West of social media poses significant risks to our society.

However, there are potential solutions that can help to tame this untamed landscape. Increased regulation, transparency from social media platforms, and education for users are just a few of the potential solutions that could help to create a safer and more responsible online environment.

Ultimately, the Wild West of social media is a reflection of our own society, with all of its strengths and weaknesses. By working together to address the challenges posed by social media, we can create a more inclusive, informed, and responsible online world that benefits everyone.

Introduction

Social media has become a ubiquitous part of our daily lives. It connects people across borders and provides a platform for communication, sharing ideas, and staying connected with friends and family. However, with its widespread adoption, social media has also brought new security risks and threats. The increasing use of social media has made it a prime target for cybercriminals, hackers, and other malicious actors. This article will explore the risks and threats associated with social media security and discuss measures that can be taken to mitigate these risks.

Types of Social Media Security Threats

1. Malware and phishing attacks

Social media platforms are often used to distribute malware and phishing attacks. Malware is malicious software that is designed to harm computer systems, steal data, or damage devices. Phishing attacks, on the other hand, are designed to trick users into giving away sensitive information such as login credentials, credit card numbers, and other personal data. Malware and phishing attacks are often distributed through links, fake websites, or messages on social media platforms.

2. Social engineering attacks

Social engineering attacks are designed to manipulate and exploit human behavior to gain access to sensitive information. Social media platforms are ideal targets for social engineering attacks as they provide a wealth of personal information about users. Attackers can use this information to create convincing scams, phishing emails, or fake websites that appear legitimate.

3. Identity theft

Social media platforms are a goldmine of personal information that can be used for identity theft. Cybercriminals can use the information available on social media to impersonate users and gain access to their financial accounts, steal their identity, or carry out fraudulent activities.

4. Cyberbullying and harassment

Social media platforms can also be used for cyberbullying and harassment. Cyberbullying involves the use of digital technology to intimidate, harass, or embarrass someone. This can have serious psychological and emotional effects on the victim.

5. Privacy breaches

Social media platforms have access to a wealth of personal information about users. This information can be misused or shared with third-party advertisers without the user's consent. Privacy breaches can also occur when user data is compromised due to security vulnerabilities on the social media platform.

Measures to Mitigate Social Media Security Risks

1. Use strong passwords

Using strong passwords is one of the easiest ways to protect your social media accounts from being hacked. Strong passwords should be a combination of letters, numbers, and symbols, and should be changed regularly. Avoid using common passwords such as "password" or "123456" as these are easy to guess.

2. Enable two-factor authentication

Two-factor authentication is an additional layer of security that requires users to provide a second form of identification before accessing their accounts. This could be a code sent to their phone or an authentication app. Enabling two-factor authentication can help prevent unauthorized access to your social media accounts.

3. Be cautious of unsolicited messages and links

Be cautious of unsolicited messages and links on social media platforms. These could be phishing scams or malware designed to steal your personal information. Avoid clicking on links or downloading attachments from unknown sources.

4. Limit the amount of personal information you share

Limit the amount of personal information you share on social media platforms. Be cautious of sharing sensitive information such as your date of birth, home address, and phone number. Also, be mindful of what you post online as this information can be used to impersonate you or carry out fraudulent activities.

Most social media platforms provide privacy settings that allow users to control who can see their posts and personal information. Be sure to use these privacy settings to limit the amount of personal information that is visible to others.

Conclusion

Social media has become an integral part of our daily lives, but it also brings new security risks and threats. Cybercriminals and hackers often use social media platforms to distribute malware and phishing attacks, carry out social engineering attacks, commit identity theft, and engage in cyberbullying and harassment. Additionally, privacy breaches can occur when user data is compromised due to security vulnerabilities on the social media platform. To mitigate these risks, users should use strong passwords, enable two-factor authentication, be cautious of unsolicited messages and links, limit the amount of personal information they share, and use privacy settings. By taking these measures, users can help protect themselves and their personal information from social media security threats.

Introduction

In today's digital age, social media has become an integral part of our daily lives. It allows us to connect with people from all over the world and share our thoughts, opinions, and experiences with others. However, with the benefits of social media come potential risks, particularly when it comes to our privacy. In this article, we will explore how to manage your social media presence and protect your privacy.

Why Privacy is Important on Social Media

Privacy is important on social media because it allows us to control who sees our personal information and how it is used. Inappropriate use of personal information can lead to identity theft, cyberstalking, and other forms of online harassment. Privacy also protects our personal and professional reputations by allowing us to maintain control over the content that is associated with our online identities.

The Risks of Sharing Too Much Information

Many people do not realize the potential risks associated with sharing too much personal information on social media. For example, posting your home address, phone number, or other sensitive information can make you a target for identity theft or online harassment. Additionally, sharing sensitive information about your employer or colleagues can lead to professional consequences, such as termination or loss of opportunities.

How to Manage Your Privacy Settings on Social Media

Managing your privacy settings on social media is essential to protecting your personal information and online reputation. Here are some steps you can take to manage your privacy settings on popular social media platforms:

1. Facebook

Facebook is one of the most popular social media platforms, and it offers a wide range of privacy settings to help you protect your personal information. To manage your privacy settings on Facebook, follow these steps:

- ➢ Click on the down arrow in the upper right corner of your Facebook profile.
- ➢ Select "Settings & Privacy" from the dropdown menu.
- ➢ Select "Privacy Checkup" to review and adjust your privacy settings.

2. Instagram

Instagram is a photo-sharing platform that is owned by Facebook. While it has fewer privacy settings than Facebook, there are still steps you can take to protect your personal information. To manage your privacy settings on Instagram, follow these steps:

- ➢ Tap the three horizontal lines in the upper right corner of your Instagram profile.
- ➢ Select "Settings" from the dropdown menu.
- ➢ Select "Privacy" to review and adjust your privacy settings.

Twitter is a microblogging platform that allows users to share short messages called "tweets." To manage your privacy settings on Twitter, follow these steps:

> ➤ Click on your profile picture in the upper right corner of your Twitter profile.
> ➤ Select "Settings and privacy" from the dropdown menu.
> ➤ Select "Privacy and safety" to review and adjust your privacy settings.

LinkedIn is a professional networking platform that allows users to connect with colleagues and potential employers. To manage your privacy settings on LinkedIn, follow these steps:

> ➤ Click on the "Me" icon in the upper right corner of your LinkedIn profile.
> ➤ Select "Settings & Privacy" from the dropdown menu.
> ➤ Select "Privacy" to review and adjust your privacy settings.

Tips for Protecting Your Privacy on Social Media

In addition to managing your privacy settings, there are other steps you can take to protect your privacy on social media. Here are some tips to keep in mind:

1. Be cautious about who you add as a friend or follower.

One of the easiest ways to protect your privacy on social media is to be cautious about who you add as a friend or follower. Avoid adding people you do not know, and be selective about the information you share with those in your network.

2. Think twice before posting personal information.

Before posting personal information, such as your address, phone number, or email address, think twice about whether it is necessary to share that information. If it is not necessary, consider keeping it private or sharing it with only a select group of people.

3. Use strong passwords and enable two-factor authentication.

Using strong passwords and enabling two-factor authentication can help protect your social media accounts from being hacked. Choose passwords that are complex and unique, and avoid using the same password for multiple accounts. Two-factor authentication adds an extra layer of security by requiring a code or token in addition to your password to access your account.

4. Be mindful of what you post and share.

Be mindful of the content you post and share on social media, as it can have a lasting impact on your personal and professional reputation. Avoid posting content that is offensive or inappropriate, and think twice before sharing content that may be misleading or false.

5. Regularly review your privacy settings.

It is important to regularly review your privacy settings on social media to ensure that you are comfortable with the information that is being shared with others. Review your settings at least once a year or whenever there are significant changes to the platform's privacy policies.

Conclusion

Managing your privacy settings on social media is essential to protecting your personal information and online reputation. By being mindful of what you post and share, using strong passwords and enabling two-factor authentication, and regularly reviewing your privacy settings, you can help keep your personal information safe and secure online. Remember, it is always better to err on the side of caution when it comes to sharing personal information on social media.

Introduction

In today's digital age, the security of our online accounts and personal data is of utmost importance. With the increasing prevalence of cyber-attacks and identity theft, it has become crucial to take necessary precautions to safeguard our online presence. One of the most important steps in this regard is to use strong passwords and two-factor authentication. In this article, we will discuss the importance of these two security measures and how they can help protect us from online threats.

The Importance of Strong Passwords

Passwords are the first line of defense against unauthorized access to our online accounts. A strong password can prevent hackers from gaining access to our personal data and sensitive information. However, many people still use weak and easily guessable passwords, which makes them vulnerable to cyber-attacks. Here are some reasons why strong passwords are important:

1. Protect Against Brute Force Attacks

One of the most common ways hackers try to crack passwords is through brute force attacks. In this method, the hacker uses a computer program to try out various combinations of letters, numbers, and symbols until they find the correct password. A strong password, which is long and complex, can make it more difficult for the hacker to crack the password through brute force.

2. Prevent Credential Stuffing

Credential stuffing is another technique used by hackers to gain access to accounts. In this method, the hacker uses a list of stolen usernames and passwords from one website to gain access to accounts on other websites. Using the same password for multiple accounts can make it easy for hackers to gain access to all your accounts. A strong, unique password for each account can prevent credential stuffing.

3. Protect Against Phishing Attacks

Phishing is a common method used by hackers to trick users into revealing their passwords. In this method, the hacker sends an email or message that appears to be from a legitimate source, such as a bank or a social media platform, asking the user to click on a link and enter their password. A strong password can make it more difficult for the hacker to guess the password even if they have access to your personal information.

Tips for Creating Strong Passwords

Now that we understand the importance of strong passwords, let us look at some tips for creating them:

1. Use a Long Password

The longer the password, the more difficult it is to crack. A password should be at least 12 characters long, and preferably longer.

2. Use a Mix of Characters

A strong password should include a mix of uppercase and lowercase letters, numbers, and symbols. Using a mix of characters makes it more difficult for hackers to guess the password.

3. Avoid Using Personal Information

Avoid using personal information such as your name, date of birth, or address in your password. Hackers can easily obtain this information from social media platforms or other sources.

4. Use a Password Manager

Using a password manager can help you generate strong, unique passwords for each account and store them securely. Password managers can also help you remember your passwords, so you do not have to write them down or reuse them.

The Importance of Two-Factor Authentication

Two-factor authentication (2FA) is an additional layer of security that can help protect your online accounts. 2FA requires users to provide two forms of authentication to access their accounts, typically a password and a code sent to their mobile device. Here are some reasons why 2FA is important:

1. Protect Against Password Theft

Even if a hacker gains access to your password, they will not be able to access your account if you have 2FA enabled. This is because they would also need access to your mobile device to enter the code sent to it.

2. Prevent Phishing Attacks

Phishing attacks can trick users into entering their passwords into fake websites. 2FA can prevent these attacks because even if the user enters their password into the fake website, they would still need to provide the additional authentication code sent to their mobile device.

3. Provide Additional Security

2FA provides an additional layer of security that can make it more difficult for hackers to gain access to your accounts. This is especially important for accounts that contain sensitive information such as bank accounts, email accounts, and social media accounts.

Types of Two-Factor Authentication

There are several types of 2FA that can be used to secure your online accounts:

1. SMS-based 2FA: This method sends a code to your mobile device via text message. You enter this code along with your password to access your account.

2. App-based 2FA: This method uses a mobile app such as Google Authenticator or Authy to generate a code that you enter along with your password to access your account.

3. Hardware-based 2FA: This method uses a physical device such as a USB key or a smart card that you plug into your computer to provide additional authentication.

Tips for Enabling Two-Factor Authentication

Enabling 2FA can significantly improve the security of your online accounts. Here are some tips for enabling 2FA:

1. Use App-based 2FA

App-based 2FA is more secure than SMS-based 2FA because it is not susceptible to SIM-swapping attacks. App-based 2FA also does not rely on the security of the mobile carrier to protect the authentication code.

2. Enable 2FA on All Your Accounts

Enable 2FA on all your online accounts, especially those that contain sensitive information such as bank accounts and email accounts.

3. Keep Your Mobile Device Secure

Your mobile device is an important component of 2FA. Keep your device secure by enabling a passcode, using a biometric authentication method, and avoiding downloading apps from untrusted sources.

Conclusion

Strong passwords and two-factor authentication are important security measures that can help protect our online accounts and personal data from cyber-attacks and identity theft. By using strong passwords and enabling 2FA, we can significantly improve the security of our online presence. Remember to use a long, complex password that includes a mix of characters, avoid using personal information in your password, and enable 2FA on all your online accounts. Stay safe online!

Introduction

As technology has advanced, phishing and identity theft have become more sophisticated and common. Phishing is a type of cyber-attack where scammers attempt to steal sensitive information, such as passwords or credit card numbers, by tricking people into providing it. Identity theft, on the other hand, involves the use of someone else's personal information for fraudulent purposes. These two types of fraud often go hand in hand, and it is important to recognize and avoid them to protect yourself from financial and personal harm.

What is phishing?

Phishing is a type of cyber-attack where scammers send emails or messages that appear to be from a legitimate source, such as a bank or a social media platform. The messages often contain a link or attachment that, when clicked, takes the victim to a fake website designed to look like the real one. The victim is then prompted to enter sensitive information, such as their login credentials or credit card numbers, which the scammers can use for fraudulent purposes.

How to recognize a phishing email

Phishing emails can be difficult to spot, but there are some signs that can help you identify them. Firstly, check the sender's email address. Scammers often use email addresses that are very similar to the legitimate ones, but with slight variations, such as "bankofamercia" instead of "bankofamerica". Secondly, check the content of the email. Phishing emails often contain urgent or threatening language, such as "your account has been compromised" or "you must act now to avoid a penalty". Thirdly, check any links or attachments in the email. Hover over the link to see the URL, and make sure it is a legitimate one. If in doubt, do not click the link or download the attachment.

How to avoid phishing

To avoid falling victim to a phishing attack, there are several things you can do. Firstly, never provide sensitive information in response to an email or message. Legitimate companies will never ask you to provide this information in this way. Secondly, always check the sender's email address, content of the email, and any links or attachments before clicking on them. If in doubt, contact the company directly using their official website or phone number. Thirdly, use strong passwords and two-factor authentication where possible to protect your accounts.

What is identity theft?

Identity theft involves the use of someone else's personal information, such as their name, address, and Social Security number, for fraudulent purposes. This can include opening new credit accounts, applying for loans, or even committing crimes in the victim's name.

How to recognize identity theft

It can be difficult to recognize identity theft, but there are some signs that can help you identify it. Firstly, check your credit reports regularly for any suspicious activity. Secondly, monitor your bank accounts and credit card statements for unauthorized transactions. Thirdly, be aware of any unexpected bills or notices, as these could be a sign that someone has opened an account in your name.

How to avoid identity theft

To avoid identity theft, there are several things you can do. Firstly, shred any documents that contain sensitive information, such as bank statements or credit card offers. Secondly, be cautious when providing personal information online, and only do so on secure websites. Thirdly, use strong passwords and two-factor authentication where possible to protect your accounts. Fourthly, be cautious of unsolicited offers or requests for personal information, and verify the legitimacy of the sender before responding.

What to do if you suspect phishing or identity theft

If you suspect that you have fallen victim to a phishing attack or that your identity has been stolen, there are several things you can do. Firstly, contact the company or financial institution involved and inform them of the situation. Secondly, file a report with the Federal Trade Commission (FTC) and local law enforcement. The FTC can provide guidance on how to report and recover from identity theft. Thirdly, monitor your accounts and credit reports regularly for any further suspicious activity. Finally, consider placing a fraud alert or freeze on your credit report to prevent further fraudulent activity.

Conclusion

Phishing and identity theft are serious threats that can result in financial and personal harm. However, by being aware of the signs and taking proactive steps to protect yourself, you can reduce the risk of falling victim to these types of fraud. Remember to always be cautious when providing personal information, to use strong passwords and two-factor authentication where possible, and to monitor your accounts and credit reports regularly for any suspicious activity. If you do suspect that you have been a victim of phishing or identity theft, act quickly to minimize the damage and protect yourself from further harm.

Introduction

Social media has become an integral part of our daily lives. It has revolutionized the way we communicate, share information, and connect with people. However, the widespread use of social media has also made it a breeding ground for scams and fraud. Social media scams are becoming increasingly common, and they can take many forms. From phishing scams to fake accounts and offers that seem too good to be true, it is important to know how to identify and avoid these scams.

In this article, we will discuss some of the most common social media scams and provide tips on how to avoid them.

Phishing scams

Phishing scams are one of the most common types of social media scams. These scams typically involve an attacker creating a fake login page or email that looks legitimate in order to trick you into revealing your login credentials or other sensitive information. This information can then be used to steal your identity or access your accounts.

One way to identify a phishing scam is to carefully examine the URL of the page you are being asked to log in on. If it looks suspicious or doesn't match the official URL of the site, it is likely a phishing scam. Additionally, be wary of any emails or messages that ask you to enter your login information or other sensitive information. If you are unsure whether an email or message is legitimate, it is best to err on the side of caution and avoid responding or clicking on any links.

Fake accounts

Fake social media accounts are another common type of scam. These accounts are often created to trick people into believing they are interacting with someone they know or trust. Fake accounts can be used to spread spam, malware, or other types of malicious content.

To avoid falling victim to fake accounts, be wary of any friend or connection requests from people you do not know or recognize. Additionally, look out for any posts or messages that seem out of character or suspicious. If you suspect an account is fake, report it to the social media platform.

Offers that seem too good to be true

Offers that seem too good to be true are a classic scam tactic. These offers often promise large sums of money, free products, or other benefits in exchange for sharing personal information or completing a task.

To avoid falling for these scams, be skeptical of any offers that seem too good to be true. Always read the fine print and do your research before sharing any personal information or completing a task. Additionally, be wary of any requests for payment or other sensitive information.

Lottery and contest scams

Lottery and contest scams are another common social media scam. These scams often involve messages or posts claiming that you have won a prize, but in order to claim it, you need to pay a fee or provide personal information.

To avoid falling for these scams, be wary of any messages or posts claiming you have won a prize. Legitimate lotteries and contests will never ask you to pay a fee or provide personal information in order to claim a prize. If you are unsure whether a lottery or contest is legitimate, do your research and contact the organization directly.

Romance scams

Romance scams are a type of social media scam that targets people looking for love or companionship. These scams typically involve someone creating a fake social media profile and using it to establish a romantic relationship with the victim. Once the relationship is established, the scammer will ask for money or other favors.

To avoid falling for a romance scam, be wary of anyone who contacts you out of the blue and tries to establish a romantic relationship quickly. Additionally, be cautious of anyone who asks for money or other favors, especially if you have never met them in person.

Investment scams

Investment scams are a type of social media scam that targets people looking to invest their money. These scams often involve someone claiming to have insider knowledge or a hot tip on a stock or investment opportunity that will yield high returns. However, these opportunities are often too good to be true and the scammer is looking to steal your money.

To avoid falling for an investment scam, be wary of any unsolicited investment opportunities or messages from strangers. Additionally, always do your own research before investing any money and be skeptical of any promises of high returns with little or no risk.

Tech support scams

Tech support scams are a type of social media scam that often involve pop-up messages or phone calls claiming that your computer or device has been infected with a virus or malware. The scammer will then offer to provide tech support or sell you a fake antivirus software.

To avoid falling for a tech support scam, be wary of any unsolicited messages or phone calls claiming to offer tech support. Additionally, never provide remote access to your computer or device to anyone you do not know or trust.

Conclusion

Social media scams are becoming increasingly common, and it is important to know how to identify and avoid them. By being vigilant and skeptical of any unsolicited messages, offers, or requests for personal information, you can protect yourself from falling victim to social media scams. Additionally, always do your own research and contact the organization directly if you are unsure whether an offer or message is legitimate. Remember, if something seems too good to be true, it probably is.

Introduction

Online harassment and cyberbullying are pervasive issues that can have severe consequences on an individual's mental health, reputation, and career prospects. As technology continues to advance and online platforms become more ubiquitous, the problem of online harassment has become more prevalent. According to a survey by the Pew Research Center, 41% of Americans have experienced some form of online harassment. This article will explore the different types of online harassment and cyberbullying and provide some practical tips for dealing with them.

Types of Online Harassment and Cyberbullying

1. Cyberstalking

Cyberstalking is the act of using electronic communication to harass, intimidate, or stalk someone. This can take many forms, including sending unwanted messages, tracking someone's online activity, or making threats. Cyberstalking is a serious crime that can have long-lasting effects on the victim's mental health and sense of safety.

2. Doxing

Doxing is the act of publishing someone's personal information online without their consent. This can include their home address, phone number, and other sensitive information. Doxing is often used as a tool for harassment and can lead to physical harm, identity theft, and other forms of harm.

3. Trolling

Trolling is the act of deliberately provoking others online by posting inflammatory or offensive messages. Trolls often hide behind fake identities and use anonymity to avoid consequences for their actions. Trolling can be particularly harmful when it targets marginalized groups or individuals who are already vulnerable.

4. Revenge Porn

Revenge porn is the act of sharing sexually explicit images or videos of someone without their consent. This can have devastating consequences for the victim, including damage to their reputation, loss of employment, and emotional trauma.

Dealing with Online Harassment and Cyberbullying

1. Do not Engage

One of the most effective ways to deal with online harassment is to avoid engaging with the harasser. Responding to their messages or engaging in arguments can often escalate the situation and give the harasser more power. Instead, consider blocking them or reporting them to the platform's moderation team.

2. Document Everything

It is essential to keep a record of any online harassment or cyberbullying that you experience. This includes screenshots of messages, emails, and any other evidence that may be relevant. This documentation can be helpful if you decide to report the harassment to the authorities or the platform's moderation team.

3. Report to the Platform

Most social media and online platforms have policies in place to address online harassment and cyberbullying. If you are experiencing harassment, consider reporting it to the platform's moderation team. Be sure to provide as much evidence as possible to support your claim.

4. Seek Support

Online harassment and cyberbullying can be incredibly isolating and distressing. It is essential to seek support from friends, family, or a professional counselor. Support groups and online communities can also be helpful in connecting with others who have experienced similar forms of harassment.

5. Take Legal Action

If the harassment is severe or involves threats of violence, it may be necessary to take legal action. This can include seeking a restraining order or pressing charges against the harasser. It is important to consult with a lawyer who specializes in online harassment and cyberbullying before taking any legal action.

Preventing Online Harassment and Cyberbullying

1. Be Mindful of What You Share Online

One of the most effective ways to prevent online harassment and cyberbullying is to be mindful of what you share online. Avoid sharing personal information such as your home address, phone number, or other sensitive information. Be cautious about the photos and videos you share online, and consider using privacy settings to limit who can see your content.

2. Set Boundaries

It is essential to set boundaries when it comes to online communication. This can include limiting the amount of personal information you share online, avoiding controversial topics that may attract trolls, and using privacy settings to control who can contact you.

3. Educate Yourself and Others

Education is critical in preventing online harassment and cyberbullying. It is essential to understand what constitutes harassment and how to recognize the signs of cyberbullying. It is also important to educate others about the issue and how to prevent it.

4. Speak Up

If you witness online harassment or cyberbullying, speak up. This can include reporting the behavior to the platform's moderation team or speaking to the person who is engaging in the harassment. It is important to let the person know that their behavior is unacceptable and will not be tolerated.

Conclusion

Online harassment and cyberbullying are serious issues that can have long-lasting effects on an individual's mental health and well-being. It is essential to be mindful of what you share online, set boundaries, and seek support if you experience harassment. It is also important to educate yourself and others about the issue and speak up when you witness harassment. By working together, we can create a safer online environment for everyone.

Introduction

In today's digital age, social media has become an essential part of our lives. We use social media platforms to connect with friends and family, share our thoughts, and even conduct business. However, with the growing popularity of social media comes an increased risk of encountering fake accounts and impersonation.

Impersonation and fake accounts can cause serious harm to individuals, businesses, and even society at large. Fake accounts can be used for a variety of purposes, such as spreading disinformation, carrying out phishing attacks, or even cyberbullying. Therefore, it is important to know how to recognize fake accounts and impersonation on social media to protect yourself and your business.

In this article, we will discuss the different ways to recognize impersonation and fake accounts on social media, along with some tips on how to protect yourself from them.

Check the account's profile picture and name

One of the easiest ways to recognize an impersonation or fake account on social media is by looking at the profile picture and name. Fake accounts often use pictures that are too good to be true or that appear to be stolen from other social media accounts. Additionally, fake accounts may use a name that is slightly different from the original account, such as adding or removing a letter or number.

To avoid falling victim to fake accounts, it is important to check the profile picture and name of any new follower or friend request before accepting it. If the profile picture seems suspicious or the name is slightly different from the original account, it is best to decline the request.

Look for inconsistencies in the account's activity

Another way to recognize fake accounts is by looking for inconsistencies in their activity. For example, a fake account may have very few followers, but they may be following hundreds or even thousands of people. Additionally, fake accounts may have little to no activity, such as no posts or only a few comments on other people's posts.

To avoid fake accounts, it is important to look for inconsistencies in their activity. If a new follower or friend request has very few followers and little to no activity, it is best to decline the request.

Check for verification

Many social media platforms have a verification process that allows users to verify their account, indicating that the account is authentic. Verification badges are usually denoted by a blue checkmark or some other symbol next to the account's name.

If you are not sure if an account is authentic or not, check to see if they have been verified. If they have, this indicates that the account is authentic and not a fake account.

Review the account's posts and comments

Another way to recognize fake accounts is by reviewing their posts and comments. Fake accounts may have posts that contain little to no text or pictures that are not related to the account's theme or niche. Additionally, fake accounts may leave comments that are unrelated or spammy in nature.

To avoid fake accounts, it is important to review their posts and comments carefully. If the posts or comments seem spammy or unrelated to the account's theme or niche, it is best to decline the request.

Use third-party tools

Finally, one of the best ways to recognize fake accounts is by using third-party tools that are specifically designed for this purpose. There are many tools available that can help you identify fake accounts and impersonators on social media.

Some of the popular tools include SocialCatfish, Hootsuite Insights, and Followerwonk. These tools can help you identify fake accounts by analyzing their activity, followers, and engagement.

Protecting yourself from impersonation and fake accounts

Now that we have discussed how to recognize impersonation and fake accounts on social media, let us discuss some tips on how to protect yourself from them.

1. Use two-factor authentication

Two-factor authentication (2FA) is a security feature that adds an extra layer of protection to your social media account. With 2FA, you will be required to enter a code in addition to your password, making it much harder for hackers to gain access to your account.

Most social media platforms offer 2FA, and it is important to enable this feature to protect your account from impersonators and fake accounts.

2. Be cautious when accepting friend or follower requests

As we have discussed earlier, one of the easiest ways for impersonators and fake accounts to gain access to your account is by sending friend or follower requests. Therefore, it is important to be cautious when accepting these requests.

Always check the profile picture and name of any new follower or friend request before accepting it. If the account seems suspicious, it is best to decline the request.

3. Keep your personal information private

Another way to protect yourself from impersonation and fake accounts is by keeping your personal information private. Never share personal information such as your full name, address, or phone number on social media.

Additionally, be cautious when sharing personal information in public forums or groups. Always check the privacy settings of any group or forum before sharing personal information.

If you come across a fake account or impersonator on social media, it is important to report it to the platform's support team. Most social media platforms have a reporting feature that allows you to report fake accounts and impersonators.

By reporting fake accounts and impersonators, you are not only protecting yourself, but you are also protecting others from falling victim to these malicious actors.

Conclusion

Impersonation and fake accounts are a serious threat on social media, and it is important to know how to recognize and protect yourself from them. By following the tips outlined in this article, you can identify fake accounts and impersonators, and take steps to protect yourself from them.

Remember to always be cautious when accepting friend or follower requests, keep your personal information private, and report any suspicious accounts to the platform's support team. By staying vigilant and taking proactive steps, you can enjoy the benefits of social media without falling victim to its dangers.

Introduction

In the digital age, protecting your personal information has become increasingly important. With the rise of cybercrime, data breaches, and identity theft, it is crucial to be aware of best practices for privacy and security. In this article, we will explore some of the most effective ways to protect your personal information and keep your digital life secure.

Understanding the Risks

The first step to protecting your personal information is understanding the risks. There are a variety of threats to your privacy and security online, including:

1. Data breaches: When a company or organization's database is hacked, your personal information may be exposed.

2. Phishing scams: Cybercriminals may use emails or text messages to trick you into providing personal information, such as your login credentials or financial information.

3. Malware: Malicious software can infect your computer or device, giving hackers access to your personal information.

4. Social engineering: Hackers may use social engineering techniques, such as pretending to be a friend or colleague, to gain access to your personal information.

5. Public Wi-Fi networks: Public Wi-Fi networks are often unsecured, making it easy for hackers to intercept your internet traffic and steal your personal information.

By understanding these risks, you can take steps to mitigate them and keep your personal information safe.

Best Practices for Privacy and Security

1. Use Strong Passwords

One of the simplest and most effective ways to protect your personal information is to use strong passwords. Avoid using easily guessable passwords, such as "password" or "123456." Instead, use a combination of letters, numbers, and symbols to create a strong, unique password for each of your accounts. You can also use a password manager to generate and store complex passwords.

2. Enable Two-Factor Authentication

Two-factor authentication adds an extra layer of security to your accounts by requiring a second form of authentication, such as a code sent to your phone or an app on your device. Enable two-factor authentication on all of your accounts to make it more difficult for hackers to access your personal information.

3. Keep Software and Apps Up to Date

Software and app updates often contain security patches that fix known vulnerabilities. Keep your software and apps up to date to ensure that you have the latest security protections.

4. Use Encryption

Encryption is a method of encoding data so that it can only be accessed by authorized parties. Use encryption to protect your sensitive information, such as your financial data or personal identification information. You can use encryption tools, such as HTTPS or a virtual private network (VPN), to protect your data.

5. Limit the Amount of Personal Information You Share Online

Be cautious about sharing personal information online. Limit the amount of information you share on social media and avoid posting sensitive information, such as your home address or phone number. When signing up for online accounts, only provide the information that is necessary and avoid giving out your social security number or other sensitive information.

6. Be Cautious of Public Wi-Fi Networks

Public Wi-Fi networks are often unsecured, making it easy for hackers to intercept your internet traffic and steal your personal information. Avoid using public Wi-Fi networks for sensitive activities, such as online banking or shopping. If you must use public Wi-Fi, use a VPN to encrypt your internet traffic.

7. Use Anti-Malware Software

Anti-malware software can help protect your computer or device from malicious software, such as viruses or spyware. Install anti-malware software on all of your devices and keep it up to date.

8. Be Wary of Phishing Scams

Phishing scams are a common tactic used by cybercriminals to steal personal information. Be wary of emails or text messages that ask for personal information or contain suspicious links or attachments. Do not click on links or download attachments from unknown sources, and verify the authenticity of any requests for personal information before providing it.

9. Use Privacy Settings

Most social media platforms and other online services have privacy settings that allow you to control who can see your information. Take advantage of these settings to limit the amount of personal information that is visible to others.

10. Monitor Your Accounts and Credit Reports

Regularly monitoring your accounts and credit reports can help you detect any suspicious activity. Review your bank and credit card statements regularly, and report any unauthorized transactions immediately. Check your credit report annually to ensure that there are no unauthorized accounts or activities.

11. Secure Your Devices

Securing your devices is an important part of protecting your personal information. Use a passcode or biometric authentication to lock your phone, tablet, or computer. Avoid leaving your devices unattended in public places and use a laptop lock when working in public spaces.

Regularly backing up your data can help protect you in the event of a data breach or device failure. Use a cloud backup service or an external hard drive to backup your data regularly.

Conclusion

Protecting your personal information is essential in today's digital age. By understanding the risks and following best practices for privacy and security, you can help keep your personal information safe from cybercriminals and other threats. Use strong passwords, enable two-factor authentication, keep software and apps up to date, use encryption, limit the amount of personal information you share online, be cautious of public Wi-Fi networks, use anti-malware software, be wary of phishing scams, use privacy settings, monitor your accounts and credit reports, secure your devices, and backup your data. With these best practices in place, you can enjoy the benefits of the digital age without putting your personal information at risk.

Introduction

In today's world, where most of our daily activities take place online, it is essential to protect ourselves from impersonators and fake accounts. Impersonators are individuals who pretend to be someone else online, often for nefarious purposes such as stealing personal information, spreading malicious content, or scamming people out of money. In this article, we will discuss the steps you can take to protect yourself from impersonators and fake accounts.

What are Impersonators and Fake Accounts?

Impersonators are people who pretend to be someone else online. They can create fake accounts on social media, email accounts, and other platforms. The intention behind creating such accounts can vary, but most often, it is done to commit fraudulent activities. Fake accounts are accounts that are not real, created to mimic genuine accounts to gain access to sensitive information. The most common types of fake accounts are those that mimic social media accounts, such as Facebook or Twitter.

Why do People Create Fake Accounts?

There are many reasons why people create fake accounts. Some do it for fun, while others do it for malicious reasons. Below are some of the common reasons:

1. To Commit Fraudulent Activities: One of the most common reasons people create fake accounts is to commit fraudulent activities. They can use the account to steal personal information, spread malicious content, or scam people out of money.

2. To Avoid Detection: Some people create fake accounts to avoid detection. This is common among cybercriminals who want to hide their identity while committing illegal activities.

3. To Harass or Bully Others: Some people create fake accounts to harass or bully others. They can use the account to post offensive content or send threatening messages.

How to Protect Yourself from Fake Accounts

1. Verify the Authenticity of the Account: The first step in protecting yourself from fake accounts is to verify the authenticity of the account. If you receive a friend request or a message from an unknown person, check their profile to see if it is legitimate. Look for signs such as profile pictures, posts, and comments. If the account looks suspicious, report it to the relevant platform.

2. Use Strong Passwords: Use strong passwords that are difficult to guess. Avoid using common phrases or words, and use a combination of letters, numbers, and symbols. Also, use a different password for each account to prevent hackers from accessing multiple accounts with one password.

3. Be Careful with Personal Information: Do not share personal information, such as your full name, address, or phone number, with people you do not know.

Impersonators can use this information to create fake accounts and gain access to your personal information.

4. Be Cautious of Phishing Scams: **Phishing scams are a common way for impersonators to gain access to personal information. They can send emails or messages that appear to be from a legitimate source, such as a bank or a social media platform. The message will often ask you to click on a link or enter your personal information. Be cautious of such messages and avoid clicking on links or sharing personal information.**

5. Use Two-Factor Authentication: **Two-factor authentication adds an extra layer of security to your account. It requires you to enter a code sent to your phone or email before you can log in to your account. This makes it difficult for impersonators to gain access to your account even if they have your password.**

6. Report Fake Accounts: **If you come across a fake account, report it to the relevant platform. Most social media platforms have a reporting feature that allows users to report fake accounts or inappropriate content.**

7. Educate Yourself: **Educate yourself on how to protect yourself from fake accounts. Keep up-to-date with the latest security trends and best practices. Attend webinars or workshops on cybersecurity and online safety.**

Conclusion

Dealing with impersonators and fake accounts is an ongoing battle. As technology evolves, so do the tactics of cybercriminals. However, by following the steps outlined in this article, you can protect yourself from most types of impersonators and fake accounts.

Always verify the authenticity of an account before sharing personal information or engaging in any type of communication. Use strong passwords and two-factor authentication to make it difficult for cybercriminals to gain access to your accounts. Be cautious of phishing scams and report any fake accounts or suspicious activities to the relevant platforms.

Remember, staying safe online is a shared responsibility. Educate yourself and your loved ones on how to protect yourselves from impersonators and fake accounts. By taking the necessary precautions, you can enjoy the benefits of the internet without compromising your security and privacy.

Chapter 11. Reputation Management: How to Clean up Your Online Presence

Introduction

In today's digital age, maintaining a positive online reputation is crucial for individuals and businesses alike. With the vast majority of people using the internet to research products, services, and even potential employers, it is important to ensure that your online presence accurately reflects who you are and what you represent.

Unfortunately, it is all too easy for negative information to spread quickly online, leaving a lasting impact on your reputation. Whether it is a negative review, a social media post taken out of context, or a news article that paints you in a negative light, these online blunders can have serious consequences.

Thankfully, there are steps you can take to clean up your online presence and protect your reputation. Here are some key strategies for reputation management:

1. Monitor your online presence

The first step in reputation management is to monitor your online presence. This means regularly checking your name and any relevant keywords on search engines and social media platforms to see what information is being shared about you.

There are various tools available to make this process easier, such as Google Alerts, which can notify you when new content is published online that includes your name or chosen keywords. Social media monitoring tools like Hootsuite and Mention can also help you keep tabs on what is being said about you on social media.

By staying on top of your online presence, you can quickly identify any negative information and take steps to address it.

2. Address negative reviews

Negative reviews can have a significant impact on your reputation, particularly if they are left unchecked. If you receive a negative review, it is important to respond in a timely and professional manner.

Start by thanking the reviewer for their feedback and acknowledging their concerns. Then, offer a solution or explanation for the issue they experienced. Even if you can not resolve the issue completely, a thoughtful response can go a long way in showing potential customers that you take feedback seriously and are committed to providing excellent customer service.

3. Create positive content

One of the best ways to counteract negative information online is to create positive content that accurately reflects who you are and what you represent. This might include publishing blog posts, creating videos, or sharing positive news articles about yourself or your business.

By proactively creating positive content, you can push negative information further down in search results and create a more accurate representation of yourself online.

4. Optimize your social media profiles

Social media is often the first place people look when researching a person or business online. As such, it is important to ensure that your social media profiles accurately reflect who you are and what you represent.

This might include updating your profile picture and cover photo, writing a compelling bio, and sharing regular updates that showcase your expertise and personality.

In addition, it is important to ensure that your privacy settings are up-to-date and that you are not sharing anything online that could be potentially damaging to your reputation.

5. Seek professional help

If you are struggling to clean up your online presence or feel overwhelmed by the task, it might be worth seeking professional help. There are many reputation management companies that specialize in helping individuals and businesses improve their online reputation.

These companies can help you identify any negative information online, develop a plan to address it, and proactively create positive content to improve your online presence.

While working with a reputation management company can be expensive, it can also be a worthwhile investment if you are concerned about the impact of negative information on your reputation.

6. Be proactive

Finally, the best way to protect your online reputation is to be proactive. This means regularly monitoring your online presence, addressing negative information quickly and professionally, and proactively creating positive content that accurately reflects who you are and what you represent.

By being proactive, you can ensure that your online presence accurately reflects who you are and what you stand for, and that any negative information is quickly addressed and mitigated.

In addition to the strategies outlined above, there are a few other things you can do to be proactive in managing your online reputation:

Build a personal website or portfolio: Having a personal website or portfolio can be a great way to showcase your skills, experience, and accomplishments online. This can help you control the narrative around your personal brand and ensure that potential employers or clients see you in a positive light.

Develop a personal brand: Developing a strong personal brand can help you stand out online and create a positive reputation for yourself. This might include developing a unique voice, sharing your expertise on social media, and consistently producing high-quality content.

Network with others in your industry: Networking with others in your industry can help you build relationships and create opportunities for collaboration and growth. It can also help you establish yourself as a thought leader and build a positive reputation within your industry.

Conclusion

Maintaining a positive online reputation is essential in today's digital age. With the vast majority of people using the internet to research products, services, and even potential employers, it is important to ensure that your online presence accurately reflects who you are and what you represent.

By following the strategies outlined above, including monitoring your online presence, addressing negative reviews, creating positive content, optimizing your social media profiles, seeking professional help, and being proactive, you can take control of your online reputation and ensure that you are presenting yourself in the best possible light.

Introduction

Social media has become an integral part of businesses, both big and small. From marketing and customer engagement to customer service and feedback, social media provides businesses with an effective way to reach out to their target audience. However, with the benefits of social media come the risks. Cybersecurity threats, online scams, and brand reputation damage are just a few of the potential dangers that businesses face on social media. In this article, we will discuss strategies for protecting your business on social media, including security and brand protection measures.

1. Develop a Social Media Policy

The first step to protecting your business on social media is to develop a social media policy. This policy should outline the dos and do nots of social media use, including guidelines for employees and brand ambassadors. The policy should also outline the consequences of violating the policy, which can range from a warning to termination of employment. A social media policy should be regularly reviewed and updated to reflect changes in the social media landscape and your business needs.

2. Train Employees on Social Media Security

Employees can be a weak link in the security chain, so it is important to train them on social media security best practices. This includes password management, recognizing phishing scams, and avoiding clicking on suspicious links. Employees should also be trained on the proper use of social media accounts, including the types of content that can and cannot be shared.

3. Use Strong Passwords

One of the most basic security measures you can take is to use strong passwords. Passwords should be complex and include a mix of uppercase and lowercase letters, numbers, and special characters. Passwords should also be changed regularly and not reused across multiple accounts. Two-factor authentication should also be enabled whenever possible.

4. Monitor Social Media Accounts

Regular monitoring of your social media accounts is crucial to catching potential threats and preventing them from causing damage. You can use social media monitoring tools to keep track of mentions of your brand or products, as well as suspicious activity on your accounts. This can include unauthorized login attempts, changes to your account information, or unusual posting behavior.

5. Limit Access to Social Media Accounts

Not everyone in your organization needs access to your social media accounts. Limiting access to only those who need it can help reduce the risk of unauthorized access or accidental posting. This can be achieved by creating separate accounts for different departments or teams and assigning specific roles and permissions to each account.

6. Respond Promptly to Security Threats

When a security threat is detected on your social media accounts, it is important to respond promptly to mitigate the damage. This can include taking down malicious content, resetting passwords, or locking down accounts. It is also important to communicate with your followers and customers about the issue and what steps you are taking to address it.

7. Use Social Media Listening Tools

Social media listening tools can help you stay on top of what people are saying about your brand on social media. This can include both positive and negative mentions, as well as potential threats or issues. Social media listening tools can also help you identify trends and opportunities for engagement with your audience.

8. Monitor Third-Party Apps

Third-party apps can pose a security risk if they are given access to your social media accounts. It is important to review the permissions granted to third-party apps and revoke access to any that are no longer needed or trusted. It is also a good idea to monitor the activity of third-party apps to ensure they are not behaving suspiciously.

9. Secure Your Mobile Devices

Mobile devices are often used to access social media accounts, which can pose a security risk if they are not properly secured. This includes using a strong passcode or biometric authentication, keeping your operating system and apps up to date, and avoiding unsecured public Wi-Fi networks.

Despite your best efforts to prevent security threats and protect your brand on social media, it is still possible that a crisis may arise. Having a crisis management plan in place can help you respond quickly and effectively to mitigate the damage. This plan should outline the steps to take in the event of a crisis, including who to notify and how to communicate with stakeholders.

Finally, it is important to stay up to date on social media trends and threats. Social media is constantly evolving, and new threats can emerge at any time. Staying informed about the latest security risks and best practices can help you stay ahead of potential threats and protect your business on social media.

Conclusion

Social media can provide businesses with a powerful tool for engaging with customers and promoting their brand, but it also comes with risks. Cybersecurity threats, online scams, and brand reputation damage are just a few of the potential dangers that businesses face on social media. By developing a social media policy, training employees on social media security, using strong passwords, monitoring social media accounts, limiting access, responding promptly to security threats, using social media listening tools, monitoring third-party apps, securing mobile devices, having a crisis management plan in place, and staying up to date on social media trends and threats, businesses can protect themselves and their brand on social media.

Chapter 13. Cybersecurity for Social Media Managers: Best Practices for Risk Management

Introduction

Social media has revolutionized the way businesses communicate with their customers. It is now an integral part of every business strategy, allowing them to reach out to a wider audience, create brand awareness, and engage with customers. However, as the use of social media grows, so does the threat of cyber-attacks. Social media managers need to take cybersecurity seriously to protect their businesses from the risks associated with social media.

In this article, we will discuss the best practices for risk management in social media cybersecurity.

Understand the Risks

The first step to effective cybersecurity is understanding the risks associated with social media. Social media platforms are vulnerable to cyber-attacks such as phishing, malware, and hacking. Cyber criminals can use social media to gain access to sensitive information, spread malicious content, and even take control of social media accounts.

As a social media manager, you must be aware of the risks and take appropriate measures to mitigate them.

Implement Strong Password Policies

Weak passwords are one of the most common ways cyber criminals gain access to social media accounts. To protect your social media accounts, it is essential to use strong passwords. Strong passwords are long, complex, and contain a combination of uppercase and lowercase letters, numbers, and symbols.

As a social media manager, you must implement strong password policies for all social media accounts. Use a password manager to store and generate strong passwords for each account.

Train Your Staff

Your staff can be your biggest asset or your biggest liability when it comes to cybersecurity. Educating your staff on the risks associated with social media and the best practices for risk management is crucial.

Provide your staff with regular training on cybersecurity best practices, such as how to identify and avoid phishing scams, the importance of strong passwords, and how to report suspicious activity.

Monitor Your Accounts

Social media is a 24/7 platform, and cyber-attacks can occur at any time. It is essential to monitor your social media accounts regularly to detect and respond to any suspicious activity.

Set up alerts for any unusual activity, such as changes in login details or unusual post activity. Use social media management tools to help you monitor your accounts and respond to any issues quickly.

Implement Two-Factor Authentication

Two-factor authentication adds an extra layer of security to your social media accounts. It requires users to provide a second form of identification, such as a code sent to their mobile phone, in addition to their password.

Enabling two-factor authentication for all social media accounts can significantly reduce the risk of unauthorized access.

Limit Access to Social Media Accounts

Limiting access to social media accounts is an effective way to reduce the risk of cyber-attacks. Only authorized personnel should have access to social media accounts. Limiting access can help prevent accidental or malicious posts, as well as reduce the risk of cyber-attacks.

Implement a Social Media Policy

A social media policy outlines the rules and guidelines for the use of social media by your staff. It can help reduce the risk of cyber-attacks and ensure that everyone is aware of the best practices for risk management.

Your social media policy should include guidelines for the use of social media, including how to handle sensitive information, how to respond to negative comments or reviews, and the consequences of violating the policy.

Back Up Your Data

Backing up your social media data is essential to ensure that you can recover your accounts in the event of a cyber-attack. Regular backups can help minimize the impact of a cyber-attack and ensure that your social media accounts can be restored quickly.

Use Social Media Management Tools

Social media management tools can help you manage your social media accounts more efficiently and effectively. They can also help you monitor your accounts for any suspicious activity and respond to issues quickly.

Social media management tools can provide you with insights into your social media performance, automate posting, and provide a central platform for managing all your social media accounts.

Regularly Update Your Software

Outdated software can leave your social media accounts vulnerable to cyber-attacks. It is essential to regularly update your social media management tools, as well as your computer's operating system and antivirus software.

Updates often include security patches and fixes that address known vulnerabilities, so keeping your software up to date is crucial to maintain the security of your social media accounts.

Be Vigilant

Finally, being vigilant is critical to effective social media cybersecurity. Monitor your social media accounts regularly for any suspicious activity and respond to any issues quickly. Stay up to date with the latest cybersecurity threats and best practices for risk management.

If you notice any unusual activity, report it immediately to your IT department or social media management team.

Conclusion

Cybersecurity is an essential aspect of social media management. The risks associated with social media are real, and cyber-attacks can have severe consequences for businesses.

Implementing best practices for risk management can help protect your social media accounts and reduce the risk of cyber-attacks. Understanding the risks, implementing strong password policies, training your staff, monitoring your accounts, and using social media management tools are all effective ways to improve social media cybersecurity.

Remember to be vigilant and stay up to date with the latest cybersecurity threats and best practices to maintain the security of your social media accounts.

Introduction

In today's world, messaging apps have become an essential part of our lives. With the increasing use of messaging apps, the need for staying safe on these apps has also increased. Although messaging apps offer convenience and help in staying connected with friends and family, they also come with some risks, such as hacking, identity theft, and cyberbullying. Therefore, it is important to be aware of the potential risks and take measures to stay safe on popular messaging apps.

Use Strong Passwords

One of the most basic yet effective ways to stay safe on messaging apps is to use strong passwords. Avoid using simple or predictable passwords such as your name or date of birth, as they can be easily guessed. Instead, use a combination of letters, numbers, and special characters. It is also important to avoid using the same password for multiple accounts. If a hacker gets hold of one password, they can access all your accounts. Therefore, use unique passwords for each account and change them periodically.

Enable Two-Factor Authentication

Another effective way to secure your messaging apps is to enable two-factor authentication. Two-factor authentication adds an extra layer of security to your account. With two-factor authentication, you will need to provide a second form of authentication, such as a code sent to your phone or email, in addition to your password. This makes it more difficult for hackers to gain access to your account.

Be Careful with Links and Attachments

Hackers often use links and attachments to spread malware or gain access to your account. Therefore, it is important to be careful with links and attachments you receive on messaging apps. If you receive a link or attachment from an unknown sender, do not click on it. If you receive a link or attachment from a known sender, verify with them if they actually sent it. Also, be cautious of shortened links, as they can be used to hide the actual URL.

Keep Your App Updated

Keeping your messaging app updated is another important step to stay safe. App updates often contain security patches that address vulnerabilities in the app. Therefore, it is important to install updates as soon as they are available. Also, make sure you download the app from the official app store. Downloading the app from unofficial sources can put your device at risk.

Use End-to-End Encryption

End-to-end encryption is a security feature that encrypts your messages, making them unreadable to anyone except the intended recipient. Many messaging apps offer end-to-end encryption, including WhatsApp, Signal, and Telegram. If you are concerned about your privacy, it is important to use a messaging app that offers end-to-end encryption. However, keep in mind that end-to-end encryption does not guarantee complete security. Hackers can still gain access to your account if they are able to bypass the encryption.

Manage Your Privacy Settings

Managing your privacy settings is another important step to stay safe on messaging apps. Most messaging apps offer a range of privacy settings that you can customize according to your preferences. For example, you can choose who can see your profile picture, last seen status, and online status. You can also choose who can add you to groups or send you messages. It is important to review your privacy settings regularly and adjust them as needed.

Report and Block Suspicious Activity

If you notice any suspicious activity on your messaging app, such as messages from unknown senders or unusual login attempts, it is important to report and block the activity. Most messaging apps have a reporting feature that allows you to report suspicious activity. You can also block users who are sending you unwanted messages or behaving inappropriately. Reporting and blocking suspicious activity can help protect you and other users from potential harm.

Avoid Sharing Personal Information

It is important to be cautious about sharing personal information on messaging apps. Avoid sharing sensitive information such as your address, phone number, social security number, or bank account details. If someone asks you for personal information, be skeptical and verify their identity before sharing any information. Also, be cautious about sharing personal information in group chats, as anyone in the group can see the information.

Be Aware of Cyberbullying

Cyberbullying is a growing concern on messaging apps, especially among teenagers. Cyberbullying can take many forms, such as harassment, spreading rumors, or posting embarrassing photos or videos. If you or someone you know is being cyberbullied, it is important to take action. Most messaging apps have a reporting feature that allows you to report cyberbullying. You can also block users who are cyberbullying you. It is important to talk to a trusted adult or seek help if you or someone you know is being cyberbullied.

Conclusion

Messaging apps have become an essential part of our lives, and staying safe on these apps is crucial. By following the tips discussed in this article, you can protect yourself from potential risks such as hacking, identity theft, and cyberbullying. Remember to use strong passwords, enable two-factor authentication, be careful with links and attachments, keep your app updated, use end-to-end encryption, manage your privacy settings, report and block suspicious activity, avoid sharing personal information, and be aware of cyberbullying. By taking these steps, you can enjoy the convenience of messaging apps while staying safe online.

Introduction

In today's digital age, social media has become an integral part of our lives. Social media platforms have provided a platform for individuals to connect, share, and communicate with people from all over the world. While social media has many benefits, it also poses significant risks to young children, such as cyberbullying, exposure to inappropriate content, and online predators. In this article, we will discuss the importance of parental controls and social media safety for kids.

The Risks of Social Media for Kids

Social media is a vast platform that can expose children to many risks. Some of the risks include cyberbullying, exposure to inappropriate content, and online predators. Cyberbullying is a form of bullying that takes place online, where children can be harassed, threatened, or humiliated. Exposure to inappropriate content can lead to psychological and emotional harm, especially for young children. Online predators can use social media to groom children for sexual exploitation, leading to severe consequences.

The Importance of Parental Controls

Parental controls are a crucial tool for parents to ensure their children's safety online. Parental controls help parents monitor and restrict their children's access to inappropriate content and online predators. Parental controls can help parents restrict access to social media, limit screen time, and track their children's online activities. These features help parents keep their children safe from harm and ensure they are using social media in a healthy and responsible manner.

How to Set Up Parental Controls

Setting up parental controls can be an easy process that varies depending on the device and social media platform. Here are some general steps to set up parental controls:

1. Identify the device or platform you want to set parental controls for.

2. Research and learn about the parental control options available for the device or platform.

3. Set up parental controls, which may include creating an account, setting up passwords, and enabling the desired features.

4. Regularly check and update parental controls as needed.

It is essential to note that parental controls are not foolproof and that parents must still educate their children about online safety and responsible social media use.

Tips for Social Media Safety for Kids

In addition to parental controls, there are several tips parents can teach their children to ensure social media safety. These tips include:

1. Keep personal information private - Children should never share personal information, such as their full name, address, phone number, or school, online.

2. Use strong passwords - Children should use strong passwords that include a combination of letters, numbers, and symbols and never share their passwords with anyone.

3. Be mindful of what is posted - Children should be cautious about what they post online, as it can be permanent and easily shared.

4. Know how to block and report - Children should know how to block and report individuals who are behaving inappropriately online.

5. Be cautious of strangers - Children should not accept friend requests from strangers or communicate with them online.

6. Take breaks from social media - Encourage children to take breaks from social media and spend time doing other activities, such as reading or playing outside.

Conclusion

Social media can be a valuable tool for connecting and communicating, but it also poses significant risks to young children. It is crucial for parents to set up parental controls and teach their children about online safety and responsible social media use. By taking these steps, parents can ensure their children's safety and well-being in today's digital age.

Introduction

Cyberbullying is a form of bullying that has become increasingly prevalent in today's digital age. With the proliferation of social media platforms, messaging apps, and other digital communication tools, bullies can now harass, intimidate, and harm their victims from behind a screen. The effects and consequences of cyberbullying can be devastating for the victims, as well as for their families, friends, and communities. In this article, we will explore the various ways in which cyberbullying can impact its victims and discuss the potential consequences that can result from this harmful behavior.

What is Cyberbullying?

Cyberbullying is defined as the use of digital communication technologies to deliberately harass, intimidate, or harm someone else. This can include sending threatening messages, sharing embarrassing photos or videos, spreading rumors or lies, and posting hurtful comments on social media platforms or other online forums. Cyberbullying can occur through a variety of channels, including text messages, emails, social media, and online gaming platforms. It can happen to anyone, regardless of age, gender, or social status.

The Effects of Cyberbullying

Cyberbullying can have a profound impact on its victims, both emotionally and psychologically. The effects can be particularly devastating for young people, who are often more vulnerable to the negative effects of bullying due to their developing brains and social skills. Here are some of the most common effects of cyberbullying:

1. Anxiety and Depression

Victims of cyberbullying may experience high levels of anxiety and depression, which can impact their mental health and wellbeing. They may feel isolated, alone, and powerless, which can lead to feelings of hopelessness and despair.

2. Low Self-Esteem

Cyberbullying can also cause a significant decrease in self-esteem and self-worth. Victims may start to question their own value and worth as a person, which can lead to a negative self-image and a lack of confidence.

3. Physical Symptoms

The stress and anxiety caused by cyberbullying can also lead to physical symptoms such as headaches, stomachaches, and sleep disturbances. These physical symptoms can further exacerbate the emotional and psychological effects of cyberbullying.

4. Social Isolation

Victims of cyberbullying may become socially isolated, as they may feel embarrassed or ashamed to share their experiences with others. This can lead to a further sense of loneliness and isolation, which can further exacerbate the emotional effects of cyberbullying.

5. Academic and Professional Impact

Cyberbullying can also have a significant impact on academic and professional performance. Victims may struggle to concentrate in school or at work, which can lead to a decline in grades or job performance.

The Consequences of Cyberbullying

Cyberbullying can have serious consequences, not only for the victims but also for the bullies themselves. Here are some of the potential consequences of cyberbullying:

1. Legal Consequences

In some cases, cyberbullying can result in legal consequences. Cyberbullying may constitute harassment, which is a criminal offense. Victims may be able to seek legal action against their bullies, which can result in fines, community service, or even jail time.

2. School or Workplace Consequences

Cyberbullying can also have consequences in the victim's school or workplace. Many schools and employers have strict policies against bullying and harassment, and bullies may face disciplinary action if caught engaging in this behavior.

3. Social Consequences

Cyberbullying can also have significant social consequences. Bullies may be shunned or ostracized by their peers, as their behavior is seen as unacceptable and harmful. This can lead to a loss of friends and social connections.

Cyberbullying can also have significant mental health consequences for the bullies themselves. Bullies may experience feelings of guilt, shame, and remorse after engaging in cyberbullying behavior. They may also experience anxiety and depression, as well as social isolation and rejection from their peers.

The consequences of cyberbullying can also have long-term effects on both the victims and the bullies. Victims may carry the emotional scars of cyberbullying well into adulthood, which can impact their relationships, career, and mental health. Bullies may also experience long-term consequences, such as difficulty forming relationships or maintaining employment, as a result of their past behavior.

How to Prevent Cyberbullying

Preventing cyberbullying requires a concerted effort from individuals, families, schools, and communities. Here are some strategies that can help prevent cyberbullying:

One of the most effective ways to prevent cyberbullying is through education and awareness. Parents, teachers, and community members can work together to educate young people about the harmful effects of cyberbullying and promote healthy communication and relationship skills.

2. Empathy and Kindness

Encouraging empathy and kindness can also help prevent cyberbullying. When young people learn to value and appreciate differences and treat others with kindness and respect, they are less likely to engage in bullying behavior.

3. Monitoring Online Activity

Parents and educators can also monitor young people's online activity to prevent cyberbullying. By staying aware of what young people are doing online, adults can intervene early if they notice any signs of bullying behavior.

4. Reporting and Intervention

Finally, it is important to encourage reporting and intervention in cases of cyberbullying. Victims and witnesses should be encouraged to report any instances of cyberbullying to parents, teachers, or other trusted adults who can intervene and address the behavior.

Conclusion

Cyberbullying is a serious issue that can have far-reaching consequences for its victims and perpetrators. The emotional and psychological effects of cyberbullying can be devastating, and the potential consequences of this harmful behavior are significant. By working together to promote education, empathy, and kindness, and by monitoring online activity and encouraging reporting and intervention, we can help prevent cyberbullying and create a safer and more respectful digital world for everyone.

Introduction

Social media has become a ubiquitous part of our lives, connecting people across the world and enabling communication and sharing on an unprecedented scale. However, with this rise in connectivity has come a corresponding rise in security threats, with hackers, cybercriminals, and malicious actors all seeking to exploit vulnerabilities in social media platforms to steal data, spread disinformation, and disrupt online communities. In this article, we will explore the emerging threats and trends in social media security and consider what the future may hold for protecting users and their data.

Overview of Social Media Security Threats

Social media platforms are a prime target for cybercriminals due to the vast amounts of personal information they contain, including users' names, addresses, phone numbers, and email addresses. Social media companies also hold valuable data on users' browsing habits, interests, and preferences, which can be exploited for targeted advertising or sold to third parties.

One of the most common social media security threats is phishing, whereby attackers create fake login pages or emails that appear to come from a legitimate source, such as a social media platform, to trick users into revealing their login details. Other common threats include malware infections, social engineering attacks, and data breaches.

Emerging Social Media Security Threats

As social media platforms continue to evolve, so too do the security threats they face. Below are some emerging social media security threats that are likely to become more prevalent in the future.

1. Deepfake Videos

Deepfake videos are artificially generated videos that use machine learning algorithms to create convincing and realistic depictions of people saying or doing things that they never actually did. While deepfakes have been used for entertainment purposes, such as creating viral memes or comedy sketches, they also have the potential to be used for malicious purposes, such as spreading disinformation or defaming individuals.

2. Social Engineering Attacks

Social engineering attacks are becoming increasingly sophisticated, with attackers using social media platforms to gather information about their targets and craft personalized messages that appear genuine and trustworthy. Common social engineering tactics include impersonating trusted contacts or authority figures, creating fake job listings or events, and using emotional appeals to elicit sympathy or urgency.

3. Data Privacy

The collection and use of personal data by social media companies is a hotly contested issue, with many users expressing concern about the amount of data that is being collected and how it is being used. While social media companies have made efforts to improve their data privacy practices, such as implementing privacy settings and offering users greater control over their data, the issue remains a concern for many users.

Trends in Social Media Security

To combat these emerging threats, social media companies are implementing a range of security measures and technologies to protect users and their data. Below are some trends in social media security that are likely to become more prevalent in the coming years.

1. AI and Machine Learning

AI and machine learning technologies are being increasingly used by social media companies to identify and mitigate security threats. For example, machine learning algorithms can be used to detect and remove fake accounts or content, while AI-powered chatbots can be used to identify and respond to potential security threats in real-time.

2. Two-Factor Authentication

Two-factor authentication (2FA) is a security measure that requires users to provide two forms of identification before accessing their accounts, such as a password and a biometric scan. While 2FA has been available for some time, it is becoming more prevalent on social media platforms as a way of mitigating the risk of account hijacking and phishing attacks.

3. End-to-End Encryption

End-to-end encryption is a security measure that ensures that messages sent between users are only readable by the sender and the recipient, preventing interception or eavesdropping by third parties. While end-to-end encryption has been available on messaging platforms such as WhatsApp, it is now being implemented on social media platforms as well, such as with the recent rollout of end-to-end encryption on Facebook Messenger.

4. Multi-Factor Authentication

Multi-factor authentication (MFA) is a step up from 2FA, requiring users to provide multiple forms of identification before accessing their accounts. For example, a user may be required to provide a password, a biometric scan, and a unique code sent to their phone. MFA is becoming more prevalent on social media platforms as a way of providing an extra layer of security to protect against account hijacking and other security threats.

The Future of Social Media Security

As social media continues to evolve, so too will the security threats it faces. Below are some predictions for what the future of social media security may look like.

1. Increased Use of AI and Machine Learning

AI and machine learning technologies are likely to play an increasingly important role in social media security, as they are able to quickly and accurately identify security threats and respond to them in real-time. For example, machine learning algorithms may be used to detect and respond to phishing attacks, while AI-powered chatbots could be used to identify and mitigate social engineering attacks.

2. Greater Emphasis on Data Privacy

Data privacy is likely to remain a key concern for social media users, as they become more aware of the amount of personal data that is being collected and how it is being used. Social media companies will need to continue to improve their data privacy practices, such as by implementing stronger encryption, offering users greater control over their data, and being more transparent about how data is being used.

3. Collaboration and Partnerships

As security threats become increasingly complex, social media companies may need to collaborate with each other and with external partners, such as law enforcement agencies or cybersecurity firms, to develop effective security strategies. This may involve sharing threat intelligence, developing joint response plans, or collaborating on the development of new security technologies.

4. Greater Use of Blockchain Technology

Blockchain technology has the potential to revolutionize social media security by providing a decentralized and secure platform for data storage and sharing. Blockchain technology can be used to create tamper-proof records of user data, transactions, and interactions, making it much harder for malicious actors to tamper with or steal this information.

Conclusion

Social media has become an integral part of our lives, connecting us to each other and to the wider world.

However, with this connectivity comes a range of security threats, from phishing attacks to deepfake videos. To combat these threats, social media companies are implementing a range of security measures, such as AI and machine learning technologies, two-factor authentication, and end-to-end encryption. As social media continues to evolve, so too will the security threats it faces, but with the right strategies and technologies in place, we can continue to enjoy the benefits of social media while keeping ourselves and our data safe.

Introduction

The increasing use of social media platforms has led to the rise of cyber-attacks, data breaches, and privacy concerns. It is, therefore, important to focus on the future of social media security, with the help of artificial intelligence and machine learning. In this article, we will discuss the potential benefits of integrating AI and ML in social media security and the challenges that need to be addressed.

The Need for Social Media Security

Social media platforms have become a primary source of communication, interaction, and entertainment for people worldwide. With the rise of social media, the risk of cyber-attacks, data breaches, and privacy concerns has also increased. Social media platforms collect and store a vast amount of personal information, including user profiles, location, browsing history, and online activities. Cybercriminals can exploit these data to conduct identity theft, financial fraud, and other malicious activities.

Moreover, social media platforms are also prone to fake news, propaganda, and misinformation campaigns that can have a significant impact on public opinion and decision-making. Therefore, ensuring social media security is crucial to safeguarding the privacy and security of users and preventing any malicious activities.

How AI and ML Can Enhance Social Media Security

Artificial intelligence and machine learning technologies have the potential to revolutionize social media security by enabling automated, intelligent, and proactive threat detection and prevention. Here are some ways in which AI and ML can enhance social media security:

1. Advanced Threat Detection

AI and ML algorithms can analyze vast amounts of data in real-time to identify patterns, anomalies, and potential threats. These algorithms can monitor user activities, detect suspicious behavior, and alert security teams to take action before any damage is done. For instance, AI can detect and block spam messages, phishing attempts, and malware-infected links, and flag any suspicious activity that may indicate a data breach.

2. Personalized User Security

AI and ML can analyze user behavior and preferences to provide personalized security measures. For example, AI can detect when a user logs in from an unfamiliar location or device and ask for additional authentication steps, such as biometric or multi-factor authentication. This way, users can have an extra layer of security that is tailored to their individual needs.

3. Data Privacy and Compliance

AI and ML can help social media platforms comply with data privacy regulations and standards, such as GDPR, CCPA, and HIPAA. These technologies can automatically identify and classify sensitive data, monitor data access and usage, and enforce data protection policies. Moreover, AI and ML can help social media platforms respond to data breaches faster and more efficiently by analyzing log data, identifying the root cause, and providing actionable insights.

4. Real-time Threat Response

AI and ML can enable real-time threat response by automating security incident response workflows. For example, when a potential threat is detected, AI can automatically trigger an incident response process that involves isolating the affected user account, disabling any malicious activity, and notifying the security team. This way, social media platforms can respond to threats faster and more effectively, minimizing the risk of data loss or breach.

Challenges in Implementing AI and ML for Social Media Security

While AI and ML have enormous potential in enhancing social media security, there are also several challenges that need to be addressed. Here are some of the major challenges:

1. Data Quality and Quantity

AI and ML algorithms require vast amounts of high-quality data to function accurately. However, social media data can be unstructured, noisy, and incomplete, making it difficult to use for training and testing AI models. Moreover, social media data can also contain biases and anomalies that can affect the accuracy and fairness of AI algorithms.

2. Security and Privacy Concerns

The use of AI and ML in social media security raises several security and privacy concerns. For instance, AI algorithms can be vulnerable to attacks, such as adversarial attacks and data poisoning, which can compromise the integrity and confidentiality of the system. Moreover, the use of AI and ML in social media security also raises ethical concerns, such as algorithmic bias, which can result in discrimination and unfair treatment of certain user groups.

3. Integration with Existing Systems

Integrating AI and ML into existing social media security systems can be challenging due to compatibility issues, technical complexities, and the need for skilled personnel. Moreover, implementing AI and ML may require significant investments in infrastructure, software, and personnel, which may not be feasible for all organizations.

4. Regulatory Compliance

The use of AI and ML in social media security must comply with various legal and regulatory frameworks, such as GDPR, CCPA, and HIPAA. However, complying with these regulations can be complex and time-consuming, as they often require significant data protection measures, such as encryption, data anonymization, and user consent.

Conclusion

The future of social media security lies in the integration of artificial intelligence and machine learning technologies. AI and ML can enable advanced threat detection, personalized user security, data privacy, and real-time threat response, which can enhance social media security and protect users' privacy and security. However, implementing AI and ML in social media security also poses several challenges, such as data quality and quantity, security and privacy concerns, integration with existing systems, and regulatory compliance. Addressing these challenges will be critical in realizing the full potential of AI and ML in social media security and ensuring the safety and security of users.

Chapter 19. The Legal Implications of Social Media Fraud and Impersonation

Introduction

Social media has become an integral part of our daily lives, with billions of people using various platforms to connect with friends, family, and strangers. However, social media has also become a hub for fraudulent activities, including impersonation, fake profiles, and phishing scams. The rise of social media fraud has prompted legal implications that must be considered to protect individuals and businesses from harm. This article will discuss the legal implications of social media fraud and impersonation, examining the laws that govern these activities and the potential consequences for those who engage in them.

Types of Social Media Fraud

Social media fraud encompasses a wide range of deceptive activities, including the following:

1. Fake profiles: Fraudsters create fake profiles on social media platforms, often using stolen or fabricated information, to engage in criminal activities such as phishing and identity theft.

2. Impersonation: Social media impersonation occurs when someone creates an account using another person's name, image, or other identifying information, with the intention of deceiving others or causing harm to the person being impersonated.

3. Phishing scams: Phishing scams are fraudulent attempts to obtain sensitive information, such as passwords or credit card numbers, by pretending to be a legitimate entity.

Legal Implications of Social Media Fraud and Impersonation

Social media fraud and impersonation can have severe legal implications for both individuals and businesses. Here are some of the potential legal consequences of engaging in such activities:

1. Criminal charges: Depending on the severity of the offense, individuals who engage in social media fraud and impersonation may face criminal charges, including fraud, identity theft, and cyberstalking.

2. Civil lawsuits: Victims of social media fraud and impersonation can sue perpetrators for damages, including financial losses, emotional distress, and reputational damage.

3. Terms of service violations: Social media platforms have strict terms of service that prohibit fraudulent activities such as fake profiles and impersonation. Violating these terms can result in account suspension or termination.

4. Intellectual property violations: Social media impersonation can also result in intellectual property violations, such as trademark infringement, which can result in legal action.

Laws that Govern Social Media Fraud and Impersonation

Several laws govern social media fraud and impersonation, including the following:

1. Computer Fraud and Abuse Act: The Computer Fraud and Abuse Act (CFAA) is a federal law that criminalizes computer-related fraud and unauthorized access to computer systems. The CFAA can be used to prosecute individuals who engage in social media fraud and impersonation.

2. The Electronic Communications Privacy Act: The Electronic Communications Privacy Act (ECPA) protects the privacy of electronic communications, including emails, text messages, and social media messages. The ECPA can be used to prosecute individuals who engage in unauthorized access to social media accounts or intercept electronic communications.

3. Lanham Act: The Lanham Act is a federal law that governs trademark infringement and false advertising. Social media impersonation can result in trademark infringement and false advertising, both of which are violations of the Lanham Act.

4. State laws: State laws also govern social media fraud and impersonation, including laws that criminalize identity theft and cyberstalking.

Consequences for Businesses

Social media fraud and impersonation can have severe consequences for businesses. Here are some of the ways that businesses can be affected:

1. Reputational damage: Social media impersonation can damage a business's reputation, as customers may be deceived into thinking that the impersonator is an official representative of the business.

2. Financial losses: Phishing scams can result in financial losses for businesses, as fraudsters may steal credit card information or transfer funds from company accounts.

3. Legal action: Businesses can sue perpetrators of social media fraud and impersonation for damages, including financial losses and reputational damage.

4. Loss of customer trust: Customers may lose trust in a business that has been the victim of social media fraud or impersonation, which can have long-lasting effects on the company's bottom line.

5. Loss of intellectual property: Social media impersonation can result in the theft of a company's intellectual property, including trademarks and copyrighted materials.

Preventative Measures

Businesses and individuals can take several preventative measures to protect themselves from social media fraud and impersonation:

1. Educate yourself: Individuals and businesses should educate themselves on the different types of social media fraud and impersonation, as well as the warning signs of such activities.

2. Use two-factor authentication: Two-factor authentication adds an extra layer of security to social media accounts, making it more difficult for fraudsters to gain access.

3. Monitor your accounts: Regularly monitoring social media accounts for suspicious activity can help detect fraudulent activities early on.

4. Report suspicious activity: Individuals and businesses should report suspicious activity to the social media platform and law enforcement agencies.

Conclusion

Social media fraud and impersonation can have severe legal implications, including criminal charges, civil lawsuits, and account suspension. Individuals and businesses must take preventative measures to protect themselves from such activities, including education, two-factor authentication, and regular monitoring of social media accounts. By taking these steps, we can mitigate the risks associated with social media fraud and impersonation and ensure that our personal and business information remains safe and secure.

Introduction

Social media has transformed the way we communicate, connect and interact with each other. With the vast reach and accessibility of social media platforms, people are constantly sharing personal information and sensitive data on these platforms. Unfortunately, this openness also makes them vulnerable to scams and impersonation. In this article, we will explore some real-life case studies of social media scams and impersonation, highlighting the methods and tactics used by scammers and how to avoid falling victim to such scams.

1. Celebrity Impersonation Scams

One of the most common types of social media scams is celebrity impersonation scams. In this scam, scammers create fake social media accounts, pretending to be a celebrity or a public figure. They use these accounts to contact unsuspecting victims, often promising them special privileges or opportunities. The scammers then ask the victim to send them money or personal information, which they can use to commit identity theft or financial fraud.

One such case involved an Instagram account that impersonated Kylie Jenner, a popular reality TV star and entrepreneur. The fake account promised a young woman a modeling contract and asked for her personal information, including her social security number. The woman fell for the scam and ended up losing thousands of dollars. In another case, a scammer impersonated Elon Musk, the

CEO of Tesla and SpaceX, and used a fake account to ask people to invest in a fake cryptocurrency.

To avoid falling victim to celebrity impersonation scams, it is important to verify the authenticity of social media accounts before interacting with them. Always look for the blue verification badge that indicates that an account is authentic. You can also do a quick search to see if the celebrity or public figure has an official social media account. Be wary of unsolicited messages, especially those that ask for personal information or money.

2. Romance Scams

Another common type of social media scam is the romance scam. In this scam, scammers create fake profiles on dating or social media sites, pretending to be someone looking for a romantic relationship. They then use these profiles to develop a relationship with their victim, often sending them love letters or gifts. Eventually, the scammer will ask for money, claiming that they need it for a personal emergency or to visit the victim.

One of the most notable romance scams involved a woman named Sarah, who fell in love with a man she met on a dating site. The man claimed to be a soldier stationed in Afghanistan and told Sarah that he needed money to pay for medical expenses. Sarah ended up sending him thousands of dollars before realizing that she had been scammed.

To avoid falling victim to romance scams, it is important to be cautious when developing relationships online. Do not share personal information too quickly and be wary of people who ask for money or gifts. Use reverse image search to check if the profile picture of your match is not stolen from someone else's account. Also, be skeptical of anyone who claims to have a sudden personal emergency that requires money.

3. Phishing Scams

Phishing scams are another common type of social media scam. In these scams, scammers create fake websites or emails that look like legitimate ones, tricking people into sharing their personal information. Phishing scams can be especially dangerous because they can result in identity theft or financial fraud.

One notable phishing scam involved a fake Facebook login page that was used to steal usernames and passwords. The fake page looked almost identical to the real Facebook login page, tricking people into sharing their login information. The scammers then used this information to access people's Facebook accounts and steal personal information.

To avoid falling victim to phishing scams, it is important to always check the URL of any website or email before sharing personal information. Look for the "https" and lock icon in the address bar to ensure that the site is secure. Be wary of unsolicited emails that ask for personal information, and do not click on any suspicious links. If you are unsure whether an email or website is legitimate, contact the company or organization directly to verify its authenticity.

4. Fake Job Scams

Fake job scams are another common type of social media scam. In these scams, scammers post fake job ads on social media sites, often promising high-paying jobs with little to no experience required. They then ask the victim to pay a fee for training or equipment, or to provide personal information for a background check.

One notable fake job scam involved a woman who responded to a job ad on Facebook. The ad promised a well-paying job as a customer service representative, but the woman was asked to pay a fee for training and equipment. She ended up paying hundreds of dollars before realizing that the job was fake.

To avoid falling victim to fake job scams, it is important to be wary of job ads that seem too good to be true. Research the company before applying for a job, and never pay money upfront for a job. Legitimate employers will never ask for money or personal information before offering you a job.

5. Tech Support Scams

Tech support scams are another type of social media scam that can be especially dangerous. In these scams, scammers pretend to be tech support representatives, often claiming to be from well-known tech companies like Microsoft or Apple. They then ask the victim to download software or provide access to their computer, which they can use to steal personal information or install malware.

One notable tech support scam involved a woman who received a phone call from someone claiming to be from Microsoft. The scammer told her that her computer had a virus and asked her to download software to fix it. The software was actually malware, which the scammer used to steal her personal information.

To avoid falling victim to tech support scams, it is important to be wary of unsolicited calls or messages from tech support representatives. Do not download software or give anyone access to your computer unless you are certain that they are legitimate. If you are unsure whether a tech support representative is legitimate, contact the company directly to verify their identity.

Conclusion

Social media scams and impersonation are unfortunately all too common in today's digital age. Scammers use a variety of tactics to trick people into sharing personal information or money, often with devastating consequences. By being vigilant and aware of these scams, you can protect yourself from falling victim to them. Always verify the authenticity of social media accounts, be cautious when developing relationships online, and never share personal information or pay money upfront for a job. By taking these precautions, you can stay safe and secure online.

"Social Media Security: Protecting Your Digital Life" is a comprehensive guidebook that aims to educate readers on the risks and threats associated with social media platforms. The book starts with an introduction to the Wild West of social media, which sets the tone for the rest of the chapters. The subsequent chapters focus on various aspects of social media security, such as privacy settings, password management, identifying and avoiding common scams, dealing with online harassment and cyberbullying, and protecting personal information. The book also covers topics such as reputation management, protecting businesses on social media, and cybersecurity for social media managers. Additionally, the book explores emerging threats and trends in social media security, including the role of artificial intelligence and machine learning. The book features real-life case studies of social media scams and impersonation, and highlights the legal implications of social media fraud. With practical tips and strategies, this book is an essential guide for anyone looking to safeguard their digital life.

ABOUT THE AUTHOR

Mr. C. P. Kumar is a retired Scientist 'G' from the National Institute of Hydrology, Roorkee, Uttarakhand, India. With a wealth of experience in his field, he has also been practicing alternative healing therapies for several years. He is skilled in Reiki Healing and Chakra Balancing with Pendulum Dowsing, and offers holistic therapy through Emotional Freedom Technique (EFT) for emotional issues. You can email Mr. Kumar at cpkumar@yahoo.com and also visit his Reiki blog at https://reiki-roorkee.blogspot.com/ for more information.